IMAGES OF ENGLAND

# THE NAILSWORTH VALLEY

IMAGES OF ENGLAND

# THE NAILSWORTH VALLEY

HOWARD BEARD

TEMPUS

*This book is dedicated to my parents and all my Nailsworth ancestors.*

*Frontispiece*: One of the Misses Hodges with a young pupil. In the early years of the twentieth century their private school, one of several in Nailsworth, was run from a wooden building in the garden of No. 5 Old Bristol Road.

First published 2005

Tempus Publishing Limited
The Mill, Brimscombe Port,
Stroud, Gloucestershire, GL5 2QG
www.tempus-publishing.com

© Howard Beard, 2005

The right of Howard Beard to be identified as the Author
of this work has been asserted in accordance with the
Copyrights, Designs and Patents Act 1988.

British Library Cataloguing in Publication Data.
A catalogue record for this book is available from the British Library.

ISBN 0 7524 3725 9

Typesetting and origination by Tempus Publishing Limited.
Printed in Great Britain.

# Contents

A light-hearted Edwardian postcard. Cards such as these were published nationally and overprinted with the name of the town or village in which they were intended to be sold.

# Acknowledgements

I would like to thank Mrs Ann Makemson, Nailsworth Town Archivist, for all her assistance and cooperation in the preparation of this book. Also Revd N. Baker, B. Bruton, R. Close, Revd J. Cull, Mrs M. Gardner, P. Griffin, M. Hemming, Mrs M. Holley, J. Keyte, I. Kibblewhite, W. Merrett, Nailsworth Town Council, the late Mrs M. Payne, N. Phillips, Mrs P. Robinson, R. Vincent, M. Weager, Mrs P. Webb. Finally, thanks to my wife, Sylvia, for all her help and advice.

# Introduction

Several books about Nailsworth have appeared over the last twenty years, notably Betty Mills' in-depth study *A Portrait of Nailsworth*. Other authors have taken different aspects of the town's past, such as the Nailsworth Railway, oral history or the work of photographer E.P. Conway. This book takes a broader look at the whole valley, not only the town itslf, but also Rodborough, Amberley, Selsley, Woodchester and Horsley.

The route chosen for exploring the photographic history of the Nailsworth Valley is as follows: firstly, Nailsworth and the hamlets nearby, then the villages on the eastern side of the valley. Continuing up the western side, the book concludes with locations further up the tributary valleys beyond Nailsworth itself.

Pictures selected for inclusion date from the 1830s through to the 1970s, with a preponderance of material from the period 1902 to 1914, for reasons explained below. Almost none of them have appeared in print before.

Clearly, before the 1850s, the only images we have of places in the valley are paintings, drawings and prints, especially the work of Stroud artist Alfred Newland Smith. From the early 1870s there exists a comprehensive series of photographs of ecclesiastical buildings, taken by Alfred's son, Oliver Smith, who had a studio in Stroud. A handful of pictures by other (mostly unidentified) photographers also survive for this period.

The 1881 census for Bath Road, Nailsworth, includes an entry for a certain Alfred Jean de Rozier, 'Photographer, Professor of Languages, Music and Drawing', born, in spite of his name, in Bavaria. However, apart from a picture in the Gloucestershire Record Office collection and one other example, almost none of his work seems to have survived.

During the 1880s, influential local families started to own cameras, with which they frequently photographed their homes and gardens. Then, in the 1890s, Paul Smith, another of Alfred Newland Smith's sons, arrived in Nailsworth, probably working in a part-time capacity, fitting in photography alongside his science teaching. Paul's pictures consist almost entirely of cabinet-size (6in x 4in) fine-definition prints pasted onto stiff card mounts. The latest known examples from Paul's camera show decorations in Nailsworth for King Edward VII's Coronation in 1902.

The year 1902, however, was also when the postcard came into its own, for it was then that the Post Office altered its regulations to allow, for the first time, the image on a card to occupy the whole of one side; previously the address to which it was being sent enjoyed this privilege, with the message and any image for which there was room sharing the reverse. So suddenly, all over Britain, photographers whose work prior to

1902 had mostly been portraiture, left their studios to capture street scenes, buildings, events, private houses and a host of other subjects, to feed the growing demand for picture postcards.

Obviously, for practical reasons, photographers tended to be somewhat territorial. E.P. Conway of Nailsworth, for example, travelling only on foot and by bicycle, covered most of the central and upper parts of the valley, while Stroud photographers worked in Rodborough and Selsley, overlapping with Conway in Woodchester and Amberley. In fact, surprisingly small places boasted their own resident photographer; for example there were two photographers each in Bisley and Chalford and others in Stonehouse, Minchinhampton, Brimscombe, Leonard Stanley and Eastington. Post offices and shops also tended to sell postcards, often the work of anonymous photographers, with only the sub-postmaster's name on them.

After the First World War private ownership of small box cameras became more common, so the need for professional photographers declined, their work being generally limited to business commissions, weddings or portraits. Copies of local newspaper photographs, recording an ever-increasing range of local events, were also now available. *Stroud News and Journal* pictures, as many people will remember, were displayed until quite recently behind glass outside the paper's office in Lansdown and could be ordered as required.

Today, of course, residents of the Nailsworth Valley, and elsewhere, mostly take their own photographs with digital cameras, video cameras and mobile phones, still, however, seeking out professionals for important occasions or difficult assignments.

Howard Beard
*September 2005*

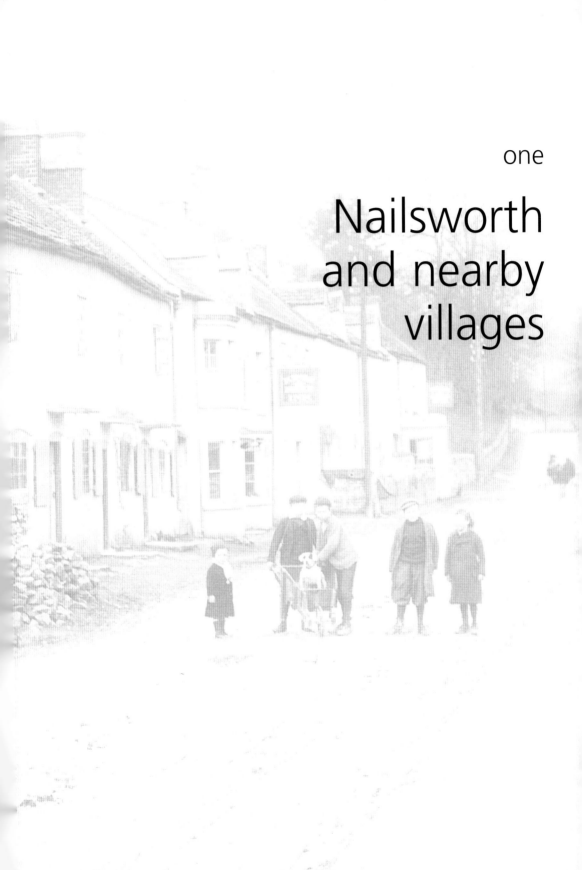

one

# Nailsworth
# and nearby
# villages

Nailsworth in 1876. This picture is one of the earliest images of the town to have survived. Note Lock's Mill, bottom left, with the 'Pepperpot Church' beyond. In the centre are the buildings of Nailsworth Brewery and, a little further away, Nailsworth Subscription Rooms. The building on the right, now the Town Hall, was at this period a Baptist chapel.

Louisa, the daughter of Vice Admiral Young of Barton End, is believed to be the artist of this 1841 pencil study of Nailsworth's first Anglican church. Built in 1794, the building was demolished in the 1890s and replaced by the present St George's Church.

Note the town clock in this photograph taken by the Chalford photographer Frank Colville, *c.* 1910. In the 1950s its bells were placed in the new clock tower put up to accommodate them at the bottom of Fountain Street. A portion of the wall in the foreground was later demolished when the war memorial was erected.

An interior view of St George's Church, taken around 1912 by E.P. Conway, Nailsworth's longest established and most prolific commercial photographer. The east end of the church looks very different today, since in 1938 the chancel, side chapel and vestries were erected 'in profound thanksgiving to Almighty God for the declaration of peace and in memory of those in our parish who fell in the war 1914-1918': somewhat ironic, one might say, in view of the fact that war was about to break out again the following year.

In Church Street was The Girls' School, now The Acorn School. In this photograph from around 1929 the pupils are, from left to right, front row: K. Hyde, M. Blake, G. Gannaway, N. Turner, M. Innis, M. Hulme, M. Jones, M. Weight. Middle row: F. Lucket, K. Ealey, N. Fletcher, C. Preston, M. Davis, K. Hannis, B. Cole. Back row: N. Tainton, W. Law, V. Hodges, V. Slaughter, E. Weight.

*Opposite above:* The vicarage and Pensile House, seen here from Wood Lane, *c.* 1910.

*Opposite below:* Drysdale's ran a plumbing, painting and decorating business from premises close to St George's Church. Here the firm is seen undertaking work at Whitecroft House, now demolished. Mr Drysdale is wearing a straw boater. Mr Furley, his plasterer, is third from the right.

*Left:* Paul Smith's picture of The Cross from around 1890 shows, from left to right, a druggist's store, F.J. Newman's ironmongery business, the post office (at its earliest known location), and the Subscription Rooms.

*Below:* The Subscription Rooms, built in 1852, once housed the Mechanics' Institute, a library on the ground floor and a lecture hall above. From around 1915 the building contained a cinema. Here, sometime in the 1950s, a queue waits to see *The Man Inside* and *The Two-Headed Spy*. For many years the Subscription Rooms were also the home of Nailsworth Boys' Club.

Building work at No. 4 Victoria Villas in 1907. In the back garden of this property stood the large wooden shed which E.P. Conway used as a studio. The house is on the corner where Bath Road meets Park Road.

Fountain Street, *c.* 1910. Looking down the street several shops can be seen, including Colwell's, which claimed to be 'the cheapest grocer', WHSmith, Green's hairdressing saloon and Antill's china shop.

The shop sign in the shape of a giant lock has hung above this ironmonger's business in Fountain Street for at least a century. At the time of this 1920s picture William Waine was the shop's proprietor.

Taylor's Garage stood in the gap in Fountain Street where today access is possible through to Old Market. This is another image from the 1920s. An earlier photograph of the same building shows a painted advertisement, where the BP sign is in this picture, announcing that the firm undertook cycle and motor repairs and was founded in 1799. One is led to conclude that, when first established, it must have been involved in some other line of business!

Warner's, who sold tobacco, were also printers. In this 1930s picture of Fountain Street, Nellie Weager stands in the doorway.

Nailsworth post office, at its third location in lower Fountain Street. Prior to this it had been sited firstly at The Cross, then in Market Street. The postman third from the left is Mr Ernie Belcher.

Fountain Street is so called because the fountain, erected in 1862 in memory of Lawyer Smith, formerly stood here. Spring Hill leads off to the left, with Bridge Street disappearing into the distance. This picture, by Paul Smith, shows decorations put up in celebration of the Coronation of Edward VII in 1902. Note the blurs where pedestrians crossed the road while the photograph was being taken.

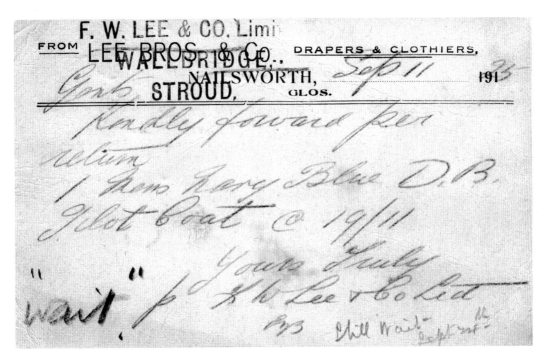

One of the shops in the 1902 photograph of Bridge Street was an outfitter's concern run by the author's grandfather. The business moved to Stroud in 1915. This trade card shows the Nailsworth address, over-stamped with the Stroud one.

By the 1920s, when this picture was taken, the former Baptist Chapel in the Old Bristol Road was occupied by Methodists. Here a church group, assembled for an as yet undiscovered event, poses to have a photograph taken.

Inside the Methodist Chapel a game takes place on a billiard table set up on what appears to be a distinctly makeshift base. Revd Hopper stands behind the young man about to cue.

The Misses Hodges, centre and right, in the garden of their home, Stoneleigh House, in the Old Bristol Road. The wooden classroom is in the background. When, in 1915, the author's mother transferred from this school to Stroud High School for Girls, she was found to be well ahead in English, but somewhat behind in mathematics! The identity of the lady on the left is unknown.

*Right:* Why E.P. Conway decided to call this very recognisable thoroughfare Witchel's Lane is unclear: it has always been correctly known as Butcher Hill's Lane. The 'Butcher Hill' in question is very probably related to a seventeenth-century Minchinhampton family of that name.

Witchel's Lane.

*Below:* Butcher Hill's Lane, in the distance, opens into Market Street. Here we see Edmonds' seed and flower shop on the left, Edward Benjamin's grocery store on the right and, beyond it, at the entrance to Brewery Lane, the Red Lion Inn. The picture dates from around 1910.

By the end of the First World War Frank Freshwater (left, seen here with his daughter, Anita), was running his family grocery business in Market Street. The frontage of the building remains virtually unchanged today, although the premises no longer function as a shop. Mr Freshwater first appeared in trade directories in 1914. By 1939 he was listed with the telephone number Nailsworth 61. A 1919 directory gives a fascinating glimpse into the town's commercial structure. In that year Nailsworth – not counting Newmarket, Inchbrook, Forest Green and Shortwood – supported eight grocers, eight public houses and hotels, six butchers and four outfitters. There were three of each of the following: coal merchants, bakers, boot and shoemakers, confectioners, insurance agents and drapers. There were two chemists, dairymen, saddlers, commercial travellers, millers, hairdressers, cycle agents, watchmakers, fishmongers, surgeons, carpenters, joiners, cabinetmakers, plumbers, blacksmiths and plasterers. There was also a tobacconist, a stationer, a wheelwright, a hay and straw dealer, a furniture broker, an auctioneer, a wool merchant, a bank, a bacon curer, a flock and bedding manufacturer, a fried fish dealer, a refreshment room, a leather-board manufacturer, a fellmonger, a solicitor, a carrier, a chimney sweep, a seedsman and florist, a newsagent, an ironmonger, a printer, a china and glass seller, a district nurse and a fancy goods dealer. A thriving and, one would think, largely self-sufficient community!

*Opposite:* Frank's daughter Ruth, left, and Sheila Warren appear here, dressed up for some dramatic or dance production in the summer of 1917.

*Above and below:* Shops at the lower end of Market Street. The upper picture, taken around 1912, shows Workman's Family, Commercial and Temperance Hotel. Beyond – by contrast – is The Britannia Inn! The lower picture shows the shops on the opposite side of the street, at the time of the 1902 Coronation of King Edward VII.

*Right and below:* For more than a century a baker's business, established by the author's great-grandfather, Samuel Allway (1835-97), existed in Cossack Square. It was continued from the 1930s by Walter Harvey. In this photograph of 1930 Walter Harvey and Leslie Pearce stand in front of the bakery, together with Florence Smith, who became Walter's wife. The children are, from left to right: Eva Watts, Vera Harvey and Paul Watts. The advertisement dates from 1933.

# ALLWAY & SON

(Proprietor: W. E. HARVEY)

**BAKERS and**

**FLOUR**

**DEALERS**

Cossack Self-
Raising Flour
a Speciality.

Best Quality
Bread, Cakes,
Etc.

*HYGIENIC MACHINE BAKERY*

**MARKET STREET, NAILSWORTH**

Lionel Bathe, who lived nearly all his life in a cottage in Brewery Lane and was a prolific amateur photographer, captured the public celebrations in Cossack Square on VE Day, 8 May 1945.

The Friends' Meeting House in Chestnut Hill, photographed in the 1920s. Worship commenced on this site in 1680. Both internally and externally it is a building of considerable charm and architectural importance.

Chestnut Hill House was, for decades, the home of one of Nailsworth's most prominent Baptist families, the Clissolds. The author's mother recalled, when visiting the house before the First World War, seeing a large trunk full of period costume, used by the family for dressing up. By 1917, when this picture was taken, it had become Dane Court School for Girls. The child on the right is holding a huge teddy bear.

Johnson's Millpond was, for many years, Nailsworth's swimming pool. In this shot from around 1940 the club hut can be seen, also the diving boards, water polo nets and areas fenced off for less experienced swimmers. Lock's Mill, then owned by B.W. Johnson & Sons, is to the right of the pond, beyond which is Barn Close and, on the left, one of several pairs of newly completed semi-detached houses in Horsley Road.

*Above:* A group of competitors and officials photographed at a swimming gala some time in the 1930s.

*Left:* Queen Mary visited Nailsworth in November 1943 from her wartime home at Badminton. She toured Johnson's factory, and is pictured here with the proprietor and his wife. Her Majesty appears to have momentarily closed her eyes as the picture was taken.

John Morris's drapery shop in George Street, decorated for King Edward VII's Coronation in 1902. It had been necessary to delay the celebrations because the King was seriously ill.

George Street, *c.* 1910. Morris's shop is seen again, beyond The George Hotel. This and The Railway Hotel were the two establishments at which travellers to Nailsworth were most likely to stay. The author's great-grandfather worked as a gardener for many years at The George. As a result of recent building development The George Hotel garden has now been replaced by residential and commercial buildings and a car park.

*Above and below*: Two interesting motorbus photographs taken by Frank Colville of Chalford. In the upper picture two vehicles, registration numbers AD1680 and AD1786, are drawn up in front of Stokescroft, in Cossack Square, next to what appears to be a large taxi. The building on the left, with the open door, is probably where they were garaged. The lower view shows AD1680 at The Cross in front of Walker's chemist shop. A notice in a window says, 'Try our 1/11 ½ corsets'!

*Above:* Watledge, seen from Forest Green, *c.* 1910. Note how E.P. Conway brought his image to life by the inclusion of a group of children.

*Below:* A second view across the valley from Forest Green. In the foreground is one of the storage ponds for Dunkirk Mill, which lies further downstream to the left and off the picture.

*Above:* The firm of Joseph Dodge & Son, established in 1851 – as this advertisement card proves – was well known in Nailsworth. By 1910 the business was in Market Street, where it stayed until closure in the 1950s. Joseph's son, Samuel, was a deacon of Shortwood Baptist Chapel and was killed in 1911, in somewhat suspicious circumstances, by a fall from an upstairs window at his home.

*Left:* Samuel Dodge, *c.* 1910.

*Above:* W.H. Davies, celebrated for his novel *The Autobiography of a Super-Tramp*, and for poems such as 'What is this life if full of care', lived for a while at this house called Yewdales, in Spring Hill. His other homes in the area were Axpills, then called Shenstone, in Cossack Square, The Croft in Nympsfield Road and, finally, Glendower in Watledge.

*Right:* One of W.H. Davies' homes, The Croft in Nympsfield Road.

Forest Green from a postcard, *c.* 1906. As Betty Mills observes in *A Portrait of Nailsworth*, this aptly named hamlet developed simply as a clearing on a wooded hillside. However, from the late seventeenth century it also became the focus of an increasingly influential Nonconformist community. In 1687 an Independent Chapel was erected. This was replaced in the 1820s, following a schism, by two further chapels, the Upper and Lower Chapels. Both are now demolished; the Upper Chapel (visible in the top left of the picture) in 1946 and the Lower Chapel in 1972. This photograph, another fine example of the work of E.P. Conway, is also of interest because it illustrates the process of residential development over the last 100 years.

*Opposite above:* The British Boys' School, 1926/27. From left to right, back row: R. Mills, R. Walker, T. Heaven, R. Tanner, N. Haines, J. Brant, B. Lemon, -?-, V. Gillman, A. Bathe. Third row: T. Healey, G. Cole, E. James, B. Davis, K. Hicks, C. Morse, H. Heaven, S. Hodges, P. Bruton, R. Turner. Second row: L. Bathe, L. Halliday, D. Drake, G. Tanner, G. Preedy (?), H. Beard, R. Woodward. Front row: B. Cowley, R. Clift, D. Joel, L. Heaven.

*Opposite below:* Back in 1938 the Headmaster of the Boys' School was an expert chess player, representing Gloucestershire. The morning after he had played a match he would set up a large chessboard on an easel and talk through his match with the school. This inevitably led to Nailsworth boys becoming familiar with, and skilled in, the game. The pupils shown here are, clockwise, left table: Eric Miles, John Bingle, -?-, ? Stephens. Middle table: Terry Morris (?), Peter Lewis, Raymond Byard, Hollis Drake, John Shepherd, Vivian Amos, Jim Turk. Right table: Bill Bruton, Ian Drew, Desmond May, Howard Brinkworth.

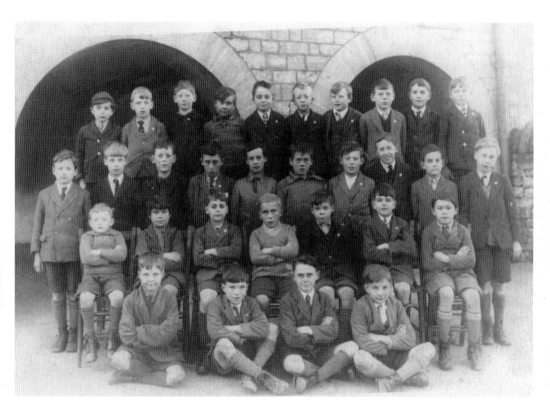

Forest Green Air-Raid Precaution wardens, 1943. From left to right, back row: A.C. Neale, B.A. Weager, V. Mills, W. Freeman, F. Pinnell, O.E. Jeffery, N. Creed, R.S. Day. Third row: F. Blake, E.J. King, O. Niblett, G.F. Jones, S.B. White, L.E. Boulton, V. Payne, F. Gannaway, C. Horwood, F. Parsloe. Second row: L. Blake, P.S. Wilmot, S.J. Webb, D.M. Horwood, L. Bennett, R.C. Timbrell (Head Warden), C.H. Burford, D. Smith, E. Bathe, F.E. Blake, P. Malpass. Front row: F.W.P. Wilmot, W. Teakle, E.S. Blake, G. Bathe, H.L. Morris.

The Forest Green ARP wardens were subjected to a particularly busy night on 27 October 1940 when around twenty-five 1kg incendiary bombs fell in their sector. The only one that caused any real damage, however, went through the roof of Grist's Flock Mill, damaging a machine and setting flock on fire. The ARP unit was also commended in February 1943 for its efficient completion of a Combined Civil Defence and Home Guard exercise.

*Opposite above:* The Upper Star Inn at Forest Green. This Stroud Brewery public house was de-licensed around 1920.

*Opposite below:* Pictured around 1907 in Northfield Road, with Inchbrook in the distance, a bread delivery boy and a couple of local children watch curiously as their photograph is taken.

Forest Green Rovers AFC Second XI, 1921/22. This team won the North Gloucester League Division II and the Stroud and District League Division III Challenge Cups. From left to right, back row: W.H. James, E. Evans, E. Beale, A. Porter, G. Iles, S. Dangerfield, G.H. Brown (hon. sec.). Middle row: A. Whiley, P. Rudge, J. Smith, D. Vines, A. Stephens, A. Bingle, O. Harrison. Front row: C. Blick, W. Freeman (captain), T. Haines.

*Opposite above:* In this mid-Edwardian photograph, both Inchbrook School and the tin church are visible at the top of the picture. The houses along the main road, including The King's Head (a Stroud Brewery public house) and Inchbrook post office, have changed little structurally today.

*Opposite below:* A second picture, from around 1906, taken at road level, shows its un-metalled surface and, curiously, a dog being given a ride in a wheelbarrow!

Stroud Rd.

Stroud Road.
569

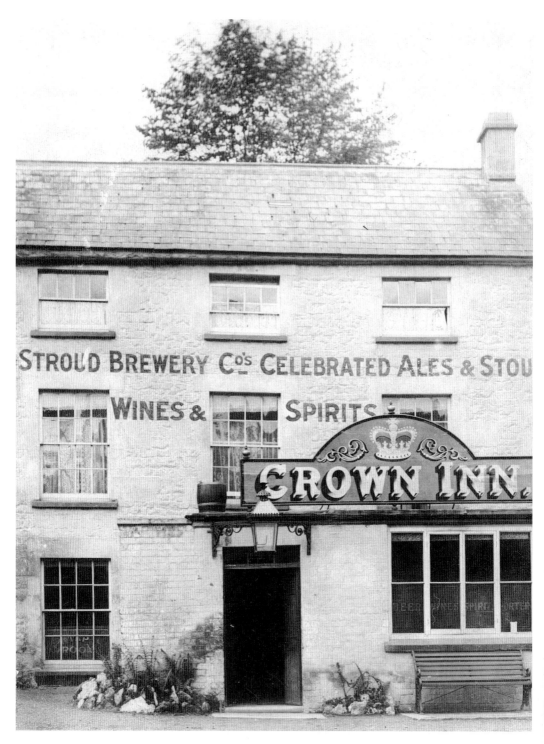

The Crown Inn at Inchbrook, *c.* 1908. Mrs Eliza Taylor was the landlady when this picture was taken. Note the large, splendidly painted inn sign. For present-day visitors to Crystal Fountain Retirement Village, this public house, currently closed, marks the point where the approach lane leaves the A46.

Newmarket, *c*. 1900. Here the full extent of Hillier's bacon-curing factory is evident. Following the closure of the business, subsequent demolition and the building of many new houses, this part of the Newmarket Valley is almost unrecognisable today.

This amusing advertisement card is one of a series published by Hillier's in the early years of the twentieth century.

A view from Shortwood towards Newmarket Road. Sent 26 July 1903, this postcard includes in its message the information that there was a 'devil of a storm last night'.

Shortwood, looking towards the cottages near the old Baptist graveyard.

An unknown Nailsworth centenarian. This postcard was produced, probably around 1910, by a little-known Nailsworth photographer, Henry S. Margrett, whose studio was in, or near, Cossack Square. The author would very much like to learn who the centenarian was.

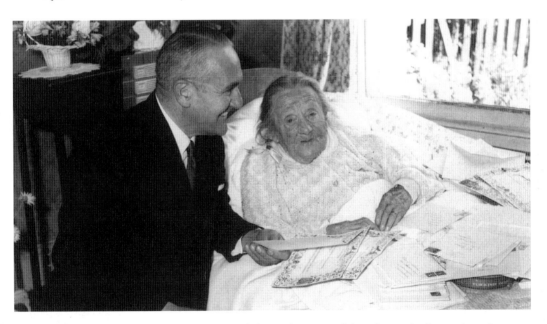

The hundredth birthday shown here is much better documented than the one in the previous picture. On 10 October 1965 Mrs Lucy Holbrow, who had spent the first ninety-two years of her life in Nailsworth, celebrated her centenary at her daughter's home in Cheltenham. Formerly a regular attendee at Shortwood Chapel, she is seen here being congratulated by the then minister, Revd Ronald Jones. Although bedridden, Mrs Holbrow still had all her faculties and was, it seems, an avid shawl knitter, donating to charity the proceeds from this activity.

This group photograph, thought to date from around 1905, is known to show members of Shortwood Chapel choir. Its location, however, is a mystery. The choir may possibly have been out of the Stroud district when it was taken, perhaps at a convention, or a missionary function. The names of those identified are, from left to right, front row seated: –?–, –?–, –?–, –?–, Evangeline Allway, Annie Ramsay, Mabel Ramsay, Lily Dodge (whose husband, Sam, was killed in 1911), Mr Antill (Choirmaster). Behind Lily Dodge is Mrs Antill, in dark clothing. Behind and to the right of her is Miss Bathe, who worked for the author's grandfather, F.W. Lee, who is seen (next to the centre pillar) wearing a straw boater. In front of him, in the dark hat, is his wife, Rose. Lower down, by the same pillar, is Walter Allway, standing partly behind his wife, Minnie.

The identification of people on images from the Golden Age of the picture postcard (from around 1902 to 1914) presents increasing problems with the passing of time. In the case of the above photograph, names were supplied by the author's mother, who lived from 1902 to 1993. Had it been discovered today, almost none would be known. Difficulties with the location of pictures can sometimes be solved by publishing them in local newspapers for readers to recognise.

*Above:* This picture, probably taken in the late 1880s by Paul Smith, then based in Stonehouse, records a trip by members of Shortwood Chapel to Tintern Abbey in the Wye Valley – a very considerable journey at that time.

*Right:* Mill Bottom Mill, now Ruskin Mill, was roofed, even in Edwardian days, with corrugated iron. It remained so until quite recently. Here, water from its extensive millpond is led out via a water wheel and sluice gate.

The Midland Trout Fisheries, a little further up the Horsley Valley, photographed just before the First World War.

The Black Horse Inn, at the top of the Bath Road leading out of Nailsworth, is now called The Tipput's Inn.

A mother and child sit on a seat at the lowest and sharpest bend of the 'W'. Note the extensive quarry spill from workings further up on the top side of the road.

At the next bend up the hill is the entrance to The Hollies. Ellen Pavey Smith, the Edwardian lady sitting in the summerhouse, may be the owner of a bath chair – just visible further inside the building. She gesticulates to her dog, Victor, to remain lying down while the photograph is taken. The summerhouse was built by the firm of G. Woodward & Sons of Watledge.

CHAMBERLAIN'S BOWLING GREEN. OPENED MAY 31ST, 1924.

*Above:* On the road from Nailsworth to Avening, behind the former Chamberlain's factory, is Nailsworth Bowling Club. The site was donated by the factory's owner, Mr E.A. Chamberlain. The picture shows the green on its opening day in 1924.

*Below:* Longfords Mill buildings are currently undergoing an extensive conversion programme from industrial to residential use. This 1911 postcard was sent to Maine in the United States, evidently for someone's collection, since no message was included.

*Above and below*: Here the mill buildings are seen on the left, with Longfords House in the distance. This postcard, of which both the front and reverse are shown, was written in German to a recipient in Lucerne, in Switzerland. It shows one of the lake's three boathouses.

Longfords Show was an annual event that ran for many years and was keenly anticipated by local people. In this picture, as the 1913 show was getting underway, ladies manned the tea tent, awaiting their first customers.

The photographer responsible for this picture of Hazel Wood, possibly E.P. Conway, obviously liked putting a lady into his foregrounds: several similar images exist, all set in rural locations around Nailsworth (see also page 127). The lady may possibly be Conway's sister, Annette.

William Mortimer, seen on the left in this family group, died in 1970, leaving a sizeable bequest to the town of Nailsworth. The money was used to fund, in his memory, the building of a room attached to the library and also to lay out the Mortimer Gardens.

A Nailsworth orchestra, photographed during the interwar years. The names of only four players are known: Hilda King, back row, far left; Ernest King, extreme right, with the cello; Mrs Gosling, seated second from left, and Helen Benjamin, middle row, third from left (wearing a black shoestring tie). It is also possible that Helen's sister, Joan, may be the cellist on the left.

This scholastic picture poses a mystery. The postcard is inscribed on its reverse, 'Nailsworth High School for Boys'. However, no one remembers such an establishment, so where it was taken, who the teacher was and how long the school lasted, remain a puzzle. All that is known for sure is that the surname of the boy nearest to the camera is Mortimer.

In order to record successive Nailsworth carnivals, E.P. Conway invariably positioned himself on the bank near the church porch. Here, fancy-dress entries parade up Fountain Street in 1912. Note the witch carrying her cauldron.

A crowd scene at The Cross. The picture was taken during a carnival in the early 1920s. Musicians from a band are visible top left. Note how almost everyone is wearing a hat.

A much later picture, probably taken in the 1950s, showing the entrance to the Big Top of a travelling circus visiting The Enochs, now known as the King George V playing fields.

In April 1978 Princess Anne came to Nailsworth from her home nearby at Gatcombe Park. Her visit included the planting of a pair of trees and, as shown here in Old Market, inspecting a guard of honour appealingly composed of undersized beefeaters from Newmarket Juvenile Club! In his welcoming speech to the Princess, Town Mayor Mr Brian Ellaway said, 'We are glad you have chosen to make your home at Gatcombe. We can assure you that Gloucestershire generally, and this town in particular, grows on one. I am quite sure you will increasingly value the quiet and peacefulness to be found here'. In her reply, the Princess commented, 'We took a while to find our home and we are very, very happy with it now'. On a walk through the town, Princess Anne was presented with a bouquet by the Butterfly Queen, Katherine Standen, and inspected an art display by the Town Hall playgroup. The following were also included in her visit: a tree planting ceremony, a local history exhibition, maypole dancing, a judo display, a tea party for sixty guests and a serenade by the Nailsworth Band.

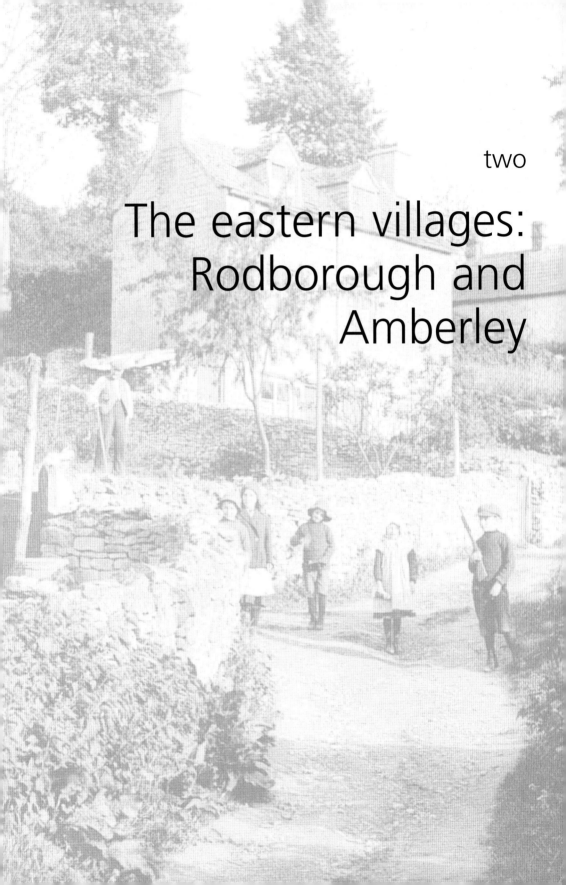

# two

# The eastern villages: Rodborough and Amberley

A boy sits on a bench on Rodborough Common. Note the absence of houses on the nearside of Walkley Hill in this picture from around 1910; also, further afield, open countryside now occupied by housing. The river Severn can be glimpsed in the distance.

Tabernacle Walk in the 1920s or '30s. The Tabernacle, far right, was built in 1766 by Thomas Adams, one of the followers of the dynamic preacher George Whitefield. It was enlarged and basically remodelled in 1837.

In spite of appearances, the history of Rodborough Fort extends back no further than 1764, when it was erected by George Hawker. It was rebuilt after 1868, on a rather grander scale, by Alexander Holcombe. Stroud's Museum in the Park contains an oil painting showing the Fort before its Victorian alterations.

Known as Fort St George, the building was run as a private boarding house around 1905. This was the dining room.

This postcard of the stretch of common land below the Fort was sent in 1922. The banner of Rodborough Church of England Sunday School dominates the right-hand side of the picture, which appears to show an open-air service. For many years May Morning celebrations have taken place closer up to the Fort itself but, to judge from the absence of daisies and the appearance of the trees, this would seem to be a summer photograph.

As this scene proves, cattle have always been present both on Rodborogh and Minchinhampton Commons. They were released each Spring on Marking Day and rounded up again in the Autumn. Spring flowers are also plentiful here, particularly the orchids. The early purple variety makes an especially impressive display, while rarer species, such as the bee orchid and fly orchid, reward careful searching.

The slopes around and below Rodborough Fort were popular, in the days before the mass ownership of motor vehicles, as one of the nearest elevated beauty spots to which the residents of Stroud could escape to take exercise or picnic. From a vantage point in the choir pews at the Baptist Chapel in the town, the author well recalls observing the area around the fort crowded with groups of leisure-seekers on warm Sunday evenings in the 1950s.

Formerly a chapelry of Minchinhampton, Rodborough has parish registers surviving only from the relatively late date of 1692. In the church's extensive graveyard are many interesting monuments, including an impressive vault belonging to the local manufacturing family of Apperly, who built Rodborough Court. Inside the church is a memorial window to Revd W. Awdry, creator of the *Thomas the Tank Engine* books, who spent the last days of his life in the parish.

The former rectory stands in grounds off Walkley Hill. It has some fine gothic windows.

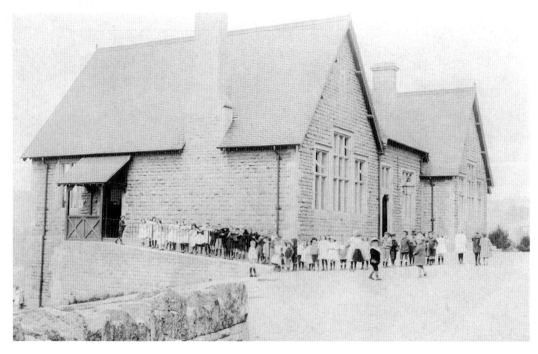

This Edwardian photograph of Rodborough School proves that the main building remains basically unaltered today. It is interesting to note that, although many of the pupils seem to realise that the picture is being taken, some do not and are walking away.

A horse and cart wait outside The Prince Albert Inn, tenanted by Amelia Cullimore at the time of this 1926 photograph.

Peace Day formally marked the end of the First World War. Here, probably in Walkley Hill, a large crowd assembles to celebrate the occasion. Note the gas lamp on the left, with its head removed and stored away for the summer season.

The village post office operated for many years from this building at the top of Rodborough Hill. It later relocated to the Bath Road and, sadly, as is so often the case these days, its postal services were recently closed down. This excellent picture, from around 1935, shows advertisements for Lyon's Ice Cream, Zebo Grate Polish, Brooke Bond Tea and the Gaumont cinema in Stroud.

Rodborough School, form 1B, 1935. Pupils are, from left to right, back row: Ronnie Neale, Graham Fletcher, Ray Temple, Alan May, Gordon Ford, Derek Pyne, Alan Haines, Ernie Blandford, -?-, John Baker. Third row: Rex Marks, Derek Smee, Bobby Everett, David Phillips (later Head of Marling School), Leonard Butcher, Ken Shelley, David Miles, Alistair Leggatt, Len Hemming, -?-. Second row: Margaret Shelton, Diana Herbert, Sheila Greensweig, Louie Holder, -?-, Mavis Berry, Pearl Weaving, Molly Smith, Sheila Ayres, Doreen Blandford, Jean Winstone. Front row: Barbara Shelton, Frances Gay, Norman Higgins, -?-, Barbara Bingle, Edna Mayo, Bert Waldron.

*Opposite above:* The 'Modern Villa' proudly advertised in this Edwardian postcard stands at the junction of Queen's Road and Coronation Road and is currently called Tara. The card belongs to an Edwardian tear-off series published by *The Stroud News*.

*Opposite below:* Before its extensive redevelopment between the wars, The Bear Hotel was a traditional double-gabled Cotswold property with a later wing attached to the rear, as this picture shows. The building survives today as the bar area of the hotel. The Bear was first recorded as an inn in 1751. Note the separate structure to the left, formerly the headquarters of the golf club that played on Rodborough Common.

MODERN VILLA, RODBOROUGH

Telephone :
No. 8, Amberley
(Glos.)

Telegrams :
Lamb, Amberley
(Glos.)

## THE BEAR HOTEL

Rodborough
STROUD
GLOS.

Proprietor :
WALTER
C. LAMB

Just up the road from The Bear in the 1930s were the Hilltop Tea Gardens. A cryptic message on the reverse of this postcard says that 'Mabel Morgan kept this café for a while – for fun'!

This well-focused picture of The Bunch of Nuts, on the parish boundary with Amberley, is enlivened by the presence of the delivery boy with his basket.

Stanfields dates from 1649 and is one of the most complete seventeenth-century buildings in the district. It derives its name from James Stanfield (for whom it was built), Lecturer of Rodborough, who was appointed by Brasenose College, Oxford, to preach in the church every Sunday.

Kingscourt, as this postcard from around 1910 proves, is an attractive hamlet within the parish of Rodborough.

In 1920 Lightpill, another part of Rodborough parish, boasted a mixed hockey club. The players, photographed here in Fromehall Park, are, from left to right, back row: N. Jones, L. Hudson, F.E. Peters, J. Shaylor, R. Mabbett, P. Davis. Middle row: Miss Wynne, C. Wilson, G. Reed. Front row: J. Hiron, G.L. Wedel (captain).

Mr C. Selwood ran his little grocery shop from the front room of a house with a bay window at the lower end of Bath Road Terrace, on what is now the main A46. The author remembers this business still in operation in the 1950s. Here Mr Selwood requests a consignment of vegetables from Bradshaw's, one of Stroud's largest greengrocery concerns.

*Above:* Moor Court, just over the border in Amberley parish, was originally a farm called Mugmore until it was substantially rebuilt, enlarged and renamed Moor Court in the mid-nineteenth century. It was for many years the home of Lord Charles Pelham Clinton, a son of the Duke of Newcastle. In later years it belonged to Mr Sydney Allen, before becoming a hotel run by the England family. It closed as a hotel in 1975. The house was subsequently divided up into flats and further buildings were erected in the grounds.

*Right:* Moor Court gardens just after the Second World War.

A young couple relax on the Common at Amberley. He reads the newspaper, while she observes him wistfully, perhaps hoping he may be a little more attentive to her! In this picture, taken in the first years of the twentieth century, note Rodborough Manor in the distance, before the disastrous fire of 1906 which left much of it in ruins.

Franked in 1903, this early postcard of locations in Amberley has a complicated history. The images are by local photographer Frank Colbourne, the card was published by Burrow of Cheltenham and was sold at Lewis and Godfrey's store in Stroud. The bell turret on the church was removed around the time of the Second World War.

*Above:* This second Burrow's postcard, of the Common above Amberley School, is equally interesting: it started as a summer picture, complete with horse and wagon, and was transformed artistically into a snow scene.

*Right:* Near the Amberley Inn, set back somewhat further from the road than its original position, stands an impressive memorial to Queen Victoria. Its nickname, 'Light and Purity', refers to the inscription on it, praising her long and glorious reign. Today the monument has neither running water nor the lamp above it.

The Amberley Inn, seen from further down the hill. The vehicles suggest a date in the 1930s or '40s. Today the hotel has an additional wing built onto its left side.

As the costume worn by this group makes clear, it is quite an early picture. It shows the Youths' Bible Class of 1897.

Amberley School, apparently in its entirety, photographed around 1905. The children all appear to be in their best clothes.

A school group from 1927. The girl third from the left in the front row is Kaye Virgo, who later taught at primary schools in the area and also ran a dance school.

The school and Queen Victoria's memorial, pictured after an unseasonably late snowfall on 24 April 1908.

Together with the banner of the Conservative Working Men's Benefit Society in the lane outside the church are, from left to right: Douglas Miles, Bert Flookes (?), Arthur Calverley (?), Ted Calverley (?), Charles Webb (?), Tom Haynes, Ray Smith, and Frank Elliott, who was for many years verger of Amberley Church.

The Old Rectory, *c*. 1908. At this time Revd Henry Summerhayes was the incumbent. The girls in his large family, some of whom appear in this photograph, all lived into extreme old age. Mercy died aged 102 and two other sisters passed away just short of their centenary. Some years ago the sisters were the subject of a television programme, *Into the Nineties*. The Old Rectory was replaced about fifty years ago by the present building.

The road from the village through Sprigg's Well and off towards Pinfarthings was still un-metalled when this picture was taken in the 1920s.

A view from the Common looking down to Sprigg's Well, with Rose Cottage in the distance. At the time that *John Halifax, Gentleman* was written, this well-known house, owned by James Guild, was rented by the book's author, Mrs Dinah Craik.

A child with a bouquet of wild flowers brings to life this Edwardian view of the houses on the upper side of Culver Hill. The scene is little changed today.

The same part of the village as the previous picture, captured back in the 1890s through the lens of P.L. Smith. As outlined in the introduction to this book, the Smiths were a talented family. According to the family tree in the possession of Stroud's Museum in the Park, Daniel Newland Smith (1791-1839), came from London. A print by him, dated 1816, is known. His eldest son, Alfred Newland Smith (1812-76), produced many drawings and lithographs, most notably a book of twenty views of ecclesiastical buildings in and around Stroud, published by J.P. Brisley in 1838. He also executed a magnificent large-scale oil painting of Stroud seen from Rodborough Fort, around 1848, which hangs on the stairs at the museum. Among Daniel's thirteen children was a younger son, Edward (1820-93), also a skilled artist with many fine pictures to his name. Alfred Newland Smith married Catherine Gough in 1833. Their son, Oliver Claude (1839-84), was a full-time commercial photographer with studios in both Stroud and Bridgwater. His work has survived in many Victorian albums, mostly in the form of portraits, but also an impressive series of views of churches completed in the early 1870s. Oliver's younger brother, Paul Lionel (1845-1932), who took the above photograph, was also responsible for a sizeable number of topographical pictures, but not, to the author's knowledge, of many portraits.

William Alder's shop at Littleworth, *c.* 1910. The board suggests that he was a butcher and grocer but, clearly, he also sold brooms, baskets, sweets and – almost certainly – a great deal more. The house is called Cornerwalls today.

This excellent picture, taken by Paul Smith around 1890, shows the original Amberley post office at Deyne Cottage on Littleworth Common, not far from The Black Horse Inn. At this time the postmistress was Mrs Mary Ann Boughton.

*Right:* Queen Mary is seen here on another local visit, this time to Littleworth House in 1941. Stanley Marling, whose home it was for many years, lived to be almost a hundred and is commemorated, along with many other members of his family, in Selsley Church. His collection of fine English furniture and other items may be seen in Gloucester City Museum, while much of his coin collection is in Stroud's Museum in the Park. The story goes that, prior to the Queen's visit, Mr Marling, knowing of her acquisitive tendencies, went through his home removing any items to which he suspected she might take a fancy!

*Below:* The information on the reverse of this photograph informs us that parish nurse Bentley is one of the ladies in the donkey cart outside the gates of Enderley House, around 1910.

Alfred Gardner, who brought up his family at Bramble Cottage, is photographed here at the wheel of his motor car in Theescombe Lane in 1910.

The Cainscross and Ebley Co-operative Society was founded in 1863, (exactly a century later the author had a summer vacation job in the society's warehouse at Ebley, putting up orders for its many village branch shops still then surviving). It was evidently felt that, in the case of this vehicle, pictured at Theescombe just before the First World War, the driver's visibility might be improved by the insertion of side windows. One wonders what the sign-writer responsible for painting the society's name on the side of the vehicle thought of this idea!

*The Hawthorns Amberley*

The Hawthorns in Lower Littleworth is an eighteenth-century building. Once a farm, it was later a hotel and is now a private house.

*Dedication Amberley War Memorial.*

For a short time in the early 1920s E.O. Reynolds ran the photographic business now known as Peckham's in Russell Street, Stroud. This is one of a series of pictures he took of the Dedication Ceremony for Amberley war memorial. The service was conducted by the Revd F.E. Warner. The Pines can be seen in the background.

Heavy snow at Amberley, March 1947. The local newspaper for 21 March reported considerable damage caused by a storm after what it described as 'the worst winter on record'. The edition recorded a blinding blizzard that had swept the hills the previous Saturday followed, after a temporary lull, by 'a tremendous gale, one of the worst within living memory'. It seems that a car had been marooned in a snowdrift at the top of Frocester Hill: two adults and a child had had to spend the night in the vehicle before being rescued by a County Council snowplough. An elm tree had fallen across the Stonehouse to Eastington road, already impassable through flooding. Other trees had blocked roads near Painswick, Minchinhampton, Woodchester and elsewhere. A Scots pine was uprooted near The Golden Cross at Rodborough, and fell across the roof of a house. Part of a heavy marble façade over a shop in King Street was dislodged, narrowly missing pedestrians below. Numerous chimney pots were blown down, windows were broken and the blind over Mr Gibson's shop in Kendrick Street was torn away. Fences were flattened, a hoarding in Wallbridge fell over, electric lights flickered, a wall at Nailsworth collapsed and, because of deep snow, there was still only one-way traffic on the Bisley to Birdlip road. Eighty-foot tall elm trees in Blakewell Lane at Painswick were torn up, together with their roots, and carried into the road in an upright position. Elderly residents of the Stroud area compared March 1947 with May 1886, when equally severe weather conditions had been experienced.

*Opposite:* Leasgill is the name of a house on the hill near Amberley post office. In this Edwardian postcard view both rider and horse seem to have spotted the photographer.

Beaudesert Park, previously known as The Highlands, takes its name from the village in Warwickshire from where the school, only established a decade earlier, moved in 1918. At the time this photograph was taken, between the wars, drill displays, organised by staff member Sgt-Maj. Miller, were a regular feature of school life. The picture shows a daytime rehearsal for an event due to take place by torchlight later in the evening.

For most of its existence, Beaudesert Park was run by three generations of the same family – the founder's grandson, J.C.P. Keyte, retired in 1995. The school, originally a boarding establishment for boys aged eight to thirteen, is now fully co-educational, with a high proportion of day pupils. In 1987 the author's wife was appointed the first Head of the Pre-Preparatory Department, opened to accommodate pupils from four to eight years of age.

# The western villages: Selsley and Woodchester

Selsley from across the Stonehouse Valley, *c.* 1910. It has been suggested that this picture was taken with a telephoto lens, surely an early use of such a device.

Quarrying has taken place on Selsley Common for centuries, as this postcard recalls. Behind Stanley Park, former home of the Marlings, is Ebley Mill where the family acquired much of its fortune. The postcard shown here was sent in 1933 by a visitor touring the area, although the picture was almost certainly taken earlier.

Stanley Park, *c.* 1910. The estate on which the Marlings built their principal home was acquired by Samuel Stephens Marling in 1850. The family lived there until 1941, when Lady Beatrice, widow of Sir Percival Marling, died. The estate was sold off at auction in 1952.

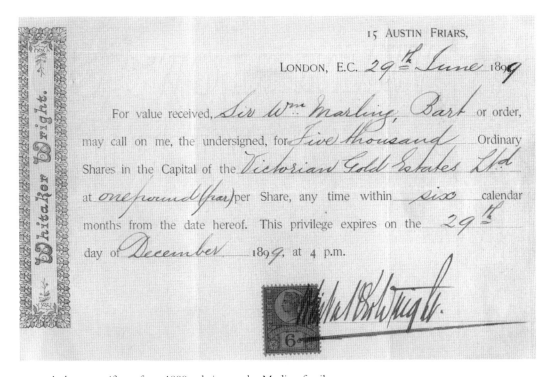

15 AUSTIN FRIARS,

LONDON, E.C. *29ᵗʰ June* 1899

For value received, *Sir Wᵐ Marling, Bart* or order, may call on me, the undersigned, for *Five thousand* Ordinary Shares in the Capital of the *Victorian Gold Estates Ltd* at *one pound (par)* per Share, any time within *six* calendar months from the date hereof. This privilege expires on the *29ᵗʰ* day of *December* 1899, at 4 p.m.

*Whitaker Wright.*

A shares certificate from 1899, relating to the Marling family.

All Saints Church was consecrated in 1862. The total cost of its construction was £3,785, most of which was donated by the Marling family, with the remaining £1,250 being raised by public subscription. The church was designed by G.F. Bodley and is well known for its fine set of stained-glass windows executed by the firm of Morris and Co. Individual windows are by Morris himself, Burne-Jones, Rossetti and Ford Madox Brown.

The church and its immediate surroundings, c. 1915.

The lych gate decorated for the marriage of Ralph Willington Yonge Radcliffe, who owned a ranch in British Columbia, and Elsie Constance Jolly of Stanley Hall, on 2 July 1907. *The Stroud News* reported that 'the stone arch at the main entrance to the church had been prettily treated with evergreens and gold and white paper festoons'. A guard of honour for the happy couple was formed by small girls dressed in pink and white and carrying shepherds' crooks decorated with flowers.

A peaceful scene at Selsley West, *c.* 1910.

Apart from the light dusting of snow that gives this picture a seasonal feel, its other point of interest lies in the tall flagpole next to the cottage.

In Edwardian days the vicar of Selsley was Revd George West, of Christchurch, Oxford. It is assumed that he is the person standing with his wife at the door of the vicarage in Selsley Hill. No longer occupied by clergy, today the building is known as Selsley Court.

This photograph of the church and school in North Woodchester is another late Edwardian picture. Kingscourt is in the background, with its little village school. In the bottom of the valley, to the right, is Woodchester Mill.

Nailsworth photographer E.P. Conway was fond of whimsical picture captions, as this 1911 picture proves. In the foreground is the millpond for Upper Southfield Mill.

Designed by S.S. Teulon, St Mary's Church was erected in 1864. It replaced its medieval predecessor that stood further north, built over the remains of the Roman villa, of which more later. St Mary's Church clock was installed in 1877, so this picture must be very early. To judge from the crinolines worn by the ladies, the un-weathered stone and the apparent total absence of graveyard monuments, it seems likely that the picture may, in fact, date from soon after 1864. The church contains several memorials transferred from the earlier building, including some to members of the Peach, Huntley and Bridges families. Rodborough Manor can be seen in the distance.

When the unidentified photographer of this school group took his picture around 1911, he seems to have been unable to fit in all he wished: there is a companion postcard overlapping this one, but including the left part of the building and more children.

This is the site of the graveyard belonging to the earlier, demolished church, with The Priory in the distance. The great Orpheus mosaic, sadly damaged in many places where graves have been dug through it, lies beneath the grass in the foreground.

*Left:* This is the only known picture of the inside of Woodchester's earlier parish church. It was taken by Oliver Smith of Stroud shortly before the building's demolition.

*Below:* Missing from the centre of the great mosaic was Orpheus, charming concentric circles of animals and birds with the music of his lyre. The picture shows an interwar opening of the pavement. The last time such an event took place was 1973, following concerns over repeated damage to the tesserae when uncovering took place. Today a replica of the complete mosaic may be seen at Prinknash Abbey.

Here South Woodchester is seen with the High Street and Baptist Chapel clearly discernable. Very few buildings have yet been built on Bospin Lane, at the top of which may be glimpsed the almshouses, demolished around 1960.

Workman's timber business, a long-established firm, had this postcard printed some time in the 1920s. Note the display of company vehicles on view. In the centre is Burrell engine number 4010, the last new traction engine supplied to Gloucestershire.

*Above and below*: Fire broke out at Workman's sawmill in the early hours of 4 August 1911. Engines from Nailsworth, Stroud and as far away as Gloucester attended. Between 1.00 a.m. and 3.00 a.m. the main buildings were gutted. Fires, of course, were common at timber yards; Nicks in Gloucester suffered a devastating blaze at roughly the same period. A series of photographs by Henry Lockyer, of Leonard Stanley, recorded the Woodchester fire. In the lower photograph Mr Workman is believed to be the gentleman in the straw hat.

*Above:* Woodchester station lay on the Midland Railway branch line from Stonehouse to Nailsworth. The cycle track currently follows its route along the valley. A poster on the station wall suggests a possible date of 1908.

*Right:* In 1960 the station building was still standing, although the line had long since closed. Today the widened A46 partly covers the station site, though the stationmaster's house survives.

*Above and below.* Two finer pictures of a sleepy village street would be hard to find – brought to life in these scenes from around 1905, of course, by people, transport and animals. In the top photograph note The Cross, one of several beerhouses in the parish. A document of 1880 records the transfer of this inn from a Mr James Cordwell to Godsell's Brewery Co. It is currently a private house. The buildings in the distance have now gone. In the lower scene a lady sits on the top of a wall, curious to see what the photographer is doing. The shop with the bay window was formerly a bakery.

When this picture was taken, around 1905, Atcombe Court was the residence of F.A. Little, JP. According to Kelly's 1910 Directory the building contained 'a curious old hiding place'. The central block, seen here, was built around 1820. A wing to the left, behind the trees, consists of an earlier structure called, firstly, The Salt Box and later Mount Pleasant.

In Atcombe Road a young man looks pensively across the valley towards Amberley. This photograph was also taken around 1905. Immediately behind the young man is a seventeenth-century house and, adjoining it, a building which, in the nineteenth century, was a dame school.

In this well-composed photograph, which has a bromide finish, a lady gazes past a cottage garden and an orchard, enjoying the same view as the young man in the previous picture.

*Opposite:* The sale particulars for Atcombe Court, when the property came up for auction in 1889. Its estate was large and reached along the top side of Convent Lane. Nearly all the buildings mentioned in the sale particulars still exist.

# WOODCHESTER,

## GLOUCESTERSHIRE,

Within half-a-mile of Woodchester Station on the Midland Railway, and 2½ miles from Stroud.

# Messrs. BRUTON, KNOWLES, & CO.

## WILL SELL BY AUCTION,

# AT THE SUBSCRIPTION ROOMS, STROUD,

## On FRIDAY, 12th day of JULY, 1889,

### AT 4 P.M. PRECISELY, IN 1 OR 4 LOTS, THE ATTRACTIVE AND COMPACT

# FREEHOLD RESIDENTIAL PROPERTY

KNOWN AS

# THE ATCOMBE ESTATE

Occupying an elevated and beautiful position at Woodchester, and comprising

## THE EXCELLENT FAMILY RESIDENCE,

KNOWN AS

# ATCOMBE COURT,

Well placed in the centre of the Estate, and commanding views of singular beauty, approached by two Carriage Drives (one with Lodge entrance), and surrounded by park-like Pasture Land, in which are an ornamental sheet of water and trout stream, Woodlands, Shrubberies, Tennis Lawns, &c., with good Stabling, Cottage for Gardener, &c.

# FARMHOUSE

AND SET OF AGRICULTURAL BUILDINGS, THREE COTTAGES FOR LABOURERS,

AND ABOUT

# 131 ACRES

Of prime Pasture, Arable, and Woodland;

ALSO

## THE INN, KNOWN AS

# "THE TEN BELLS,"

And the PRIVATE DWELLING-HOUSE and THREE COTTAGES adjoining.

POSSESSION OF THE RESIDENCE AND LAND WILL BE GIVEN ON COMPLETION OF THE PURCHASE.

Particulars and Plans may be obtained of Messrs. LITTLE & MILLS, Solicitors, Stroud; or the AUCTIONEERS, Albion Chambers, Gloucester.

FROGMARSH

These cottages at Summerwells have disappeared, replaced by newer houses. What a superb piece of social history this is. A carrier has paused in the roadway and the cottagers have come out to have their photograph taken – girls in aprons and working men in caps, jackets, waistcoats and sturdy boots; one leans against a wall, smoking his pipe. Water from the roof is collected in a tin bath and a canary cage hangs over the doorway for its occupant to enjoy some fresh air.

*Opposite above and below:* Two Edwardian pictures of Frogmarsh. Note, on the right of the upper photograph, the summerhouse associated with Frogmarsh Mill. In 1938 architectural features from this classical garden house, built around 1720, were removed and incorporated by Lord Aberconway into a replica at Bodnant in North Wales. The core of the summerhouse at Woodchester remained standing and was used successively as a boiler house and offices. Part of the double-gabled building next to it, and the mill chimney, have now gone. In the lower picture, behind the wool-drying tower, is the former public house, The Ten Bells.

Near Summerwells is the Franciscan Convent of the Immaculate Conception, completed in 1865. In 1910 it was occupied by an abbess and twenty-seven sisters. It was also responsible for an orphanage containing more than twenty children.

The church of the Dominican Priory, opened in 1849, is further along the road towards Nailsworth. It contains the alabaster tomb of its founder, William Leigh of Woodchester Park. The Priory's domestic buildings were demolished in 1970.

The dedication of the Wayside Memorial Cross, on the slope below the Catholic church, took place at the end of July 1921. Among those it commemorates is George Archer-Shee, upon whose story Terence Rattigan based *The Winslow Boy*. George was killed in action on 31 October 1914 at the age of nineteen. The Cross was dedicated on 3 June 1917, when the war was still far from over, making it one of the earliest war memorials in the country. Curiously, a day or two before the dedication was due to take place, it was discovered that the figure of Christ had been lost in transit by the railway company conveying it to Woodchester. It was temporarily replaced by one earlier donated to The Priory by W.E. Gladstone's sister.

Woodchester Mansion is a time capsule. This magnificent mid-nineteenth century masterpiece, designed by local architect Benjamin Bucknall, was abandoned around 1870, roofed and with its servants' quarters complete, but otherwise internally unfinished. A builder's ladder remained leaning against a wall.

*Above and below:* These amateur photographs were taken around the time of the First World War and appear to show an event taking place by the Woodchester Mansion, with horse jumps and children's swing boats.

*Above and below:* A series of postcards was produced around 1904, recording life on the Woodchester Park Estate. Here are two pictures from that series. The boathouse dates from around 1820 and belongs to the earlier house, called Spring Park, which was replaced by the mansion.

For this photograph we have, uncommonly, an exact date, 7 September 1901. The working horse is believed to be on the lower entrance drive to Woodchester Park. For many years both the park and the mansion were closed to the public, although in Edwardian times the grounds were evidently used for events and casual walks – the author's grandmother visited the mansion on several occasions around 1910. When in recent years, thanks to the National Trust, it became possible once again to explore the series of five lakes that descend through glorious unspoilt scenery down towards Inchbrook, the people of Stroud realised what they had been missing for so long.

This image would appeal to collectors of several different kinds of photograph. Firstly, and most obviously, it would be sought by enthusiasts interested in topographical pictures of Woodchester. It might, however, also appear in a specialist dealer's stock under the headings of 'social history', 'rural' life' or 'animals'.

*Above:* A Newman and Henders Christmas whist drive and dance in the YMCA hut at Woodchester, which was burnt down during the Second World War shortly after this photograph was taken.

*Right:* The gardener at Woodchester Lodge was apparently a keen chrysanthemum grower. Woodchester Lodge is believed to have been the lower access point for Rodborough Manor. It was transferred to Woodchester parish in 1990.

# NEWMAN, HENDER & CO., LTD.

### SPECIALISTS IN THE MANUFACTURE OF BRASS, GUNMETAL AND IRON VALVES, COCKS AND GENERAL STEAM AND WATER FITTINGS.

TRADE MARK

TELEGRAMS:
NEWMAN, WOODCHESTER.
TELEPHONE:
66 & 67 NAILSWORTH.
CODES
A.B.C. 5TH EDITION
BENTLEY'S
SECOND PHRASE CODE.

TRADE MARK

LONDON OFFICE:
BRITISH INDUSTRIES HOUSE,
Nº 9. ENGINEERING SECTION,
MARBLE ARCH, W.I.
TELEPHONE:
MAYFAIR 2188
TELEGRAMS:
FULWAVAL, WESDO,
LONDON.

### WOODCHESTER GLOS. ENGLAND

YOURS
OURS RSB/MB

30th September, 1937.

Messrs. Dexters Ltd.,
2, 4 & 8, Park Road,
WELLINGBOROUGH.

*Above and below:* Two business letterheads from the 1930s. The upper one was issued by Newman and Henders, of Dyehouse Mill, the firm whose whist drive is shown on page 107. S.J. Newman founded his engineering business on this site in 1879 and in 1896 it became Newman Hender and Co., specialising in the manufacture of engine fittings, gun-metal and valves. Below is the letterhead of Matthew Grist's flock factory at Merrett's Mill. The Grists came to Gloucestershire from Somerset around 1800. Settling initially at Stonehouse, they later converted a number of mills to flock production, notably at Rooksmoor, Brimscombe and Woodchester. It would be fair to say that the illustrations on both letterheads are somewhat idealised artists' impressions of the buildings the factories occupied.

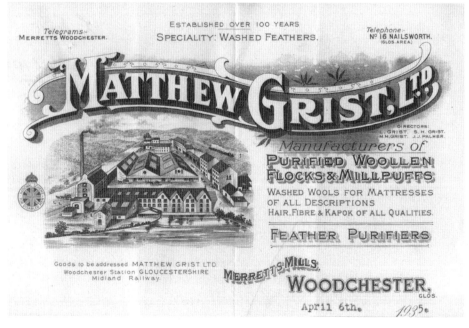

# four

# The villages upstream: Avening and Horsley

Avening nestles at the junction of several tributary valleys that feed their streams down the Aven Brook, via Longfords Lake, into Nailsworth.

Avening's main street runs from left to right in this picture, with The Cross Inn visible at the point where the road to Tetbury is seen ascending the hill. On the opposite side of the road from The Cross Inn is The Sawyer's Arms, demolished for road widening in the late 1950s.

Holy Cross Parish Church has many surviving Norman features. The building was partially restored in 1887 and again underwent substantial repair work between 1903 and 1906. It has early parish registers commencing in 1557. When the author was a child there was, in the south transept, a small museum which included a human skeleton and a stone coffin.

The school, on the left, was built in 1842 and enlarged in 1893. A rather self-conscious handful of pupils provide a pleasing foreground for this Edwardian view by Mark Merrett of Stroud.

A lady cyclist prepares to mount her bicycle outside The Cross Inn, *c.* 1910. As the sign makes clear, the public house was served by the Stroud Brewery Co.

The village street in Edwardian days. The shop premises on the right were those of The Cotswold Stores. At a later date there was also a haberdashery slightly nearer to where the photographer was standing. Note the tyre marks on the un-surfaced road. The postcard, heavily tinted, is intended to suggest a primitive form of colour photography.

Avening Baptist Chapel, capable of seating 200 people, was built in 1806 and enlarged in 1821. In the eighteenth century the Nailsworth area became one of the most active nationally in terms of the Baptist cause. The main reason for this success was Shortwood's dynamic pastor, Benjamin Francis. Unfortunately, the fact that Shortwood Chapel was established in 1715, but its registers survive only from a century later, has caused many problems for those with local Baptist ancestry wishing to trace their forebears. Avening Baptist Chapel has now been redeveloped as six flats.

On the reverse of this picture are the words, 'Farmers shoot at Avening. Mr Martin in the middle'. Note the terrier, the spades and the pair of ferrets.

A group of village schoolchildren photographed, it is thought, between 1928 and 1930. The teacher is Mrs Mabel Fletcher. Those pupils whose names are known are, from left to right, front row: Bill Chip, -?-, Arthur Pope, Bernard Godwin, -?-, Owen Fletcher, Jim Pope. Second row: Stella Coates (third from left), May Fletcher (fourth), Margery Clark (fifth). Third row: Walter Clark (first from left), Molly Clapton (fourth), Betty Bolland (fifth). Back row: Bill Fletcher (second boy from left).

Nag's Head is an attractive hamlet about a mile east of Avening. Its houses have some interesting architectural features. Nag's Head presumably takes its name from the public house, kept by Albert Boulton in 1910. The building seen bottom left was a flour mill.

A family stands in front of Rodway Place, a fine early Avening property. The date of the photograph is 1908.

PHOTO.
B. MAY
AVENING

St Martin's Church, Horsley. This lithograph by Alfred Smith was executed in the 1830s and was included in his collection of prints of ecclesiastical buildings in the Stroud area published in 1838. The reason it is significant is because it shows the church just before the nave and chancel were rebuilt. Note the exterior flight of steps, the windows dating from various periods and the dormers set into the roof. The tower, dating from around 1380, was left alone in the reconstruction and remains substantially unaltered today. Alfred Smith's book of lithographs sold for 21s a copy (15s to subscribers), a considerable sum at that time. Profits from the sale of the book, dedicated to the Bishop of Gloucester and Bristol, were intended to go towards a fund to rebuild Stroud Parish Church. However, this did not, in fact, happen until nearly thirty years later.

*Opposite:* This charming postcard by the Avening photographer Bertrand May was sent to an address in Essex in August 1907. On the reverse is written the message 'Do you want a little washerwoman?' Bertrand May was in his early twenties when this photograph was taken. His work is not common and, apart from Avening, he appears to have photographed only villages adjacent to the parish.

E.P. Conway enjoyed creating composite pictures to be used as Christmas cards. Here, for Horsley, he has combined five cards with festive holly and ivy, then added a greeting in his own highly distinctive handwriting. Similar cards exist for other locations, including Nailsworth, Minchinhampton, Amberley, Kingscote and Hyde. For the collector, owning the composite postcard indicates the separate cards that may, perhaps, be discovered later as individuals.

Still with the festive season in mind, another greetings card, created around 1910, for the owners of The Priory.

Horsley Priory and Village. 1099

Conway's distant view of Horsley, taken around 1909, shows The Priory on the left and the church in the centre. To the right are properties along, or near, the village street.

Horsley's war memorial, unveiled in July 1921, formerly stood at the top of the hill leading up from Nailsworth. The photograph records part of the dedication service for this monument. Outbuildings belonging to Horsley Court can be seen in the background.

*Above and below:* Two complementary photographs of the village street, both taken around 1910, but looking in opposite directions. In the top picture the school is prominent, with pupils assembled in the road outside. In the lower view note The Bell and Castle public house.

*Above and below:* St Martin's Church, rebuilt around 1840, was further restored in 1887 at a cost of £642. Before Nailsworth's creation as a separate parish just over a century ago, much of the town, together with several nearby hamlets, was included in Horsley parish. The main changes that have taken place inside St Martin's Church over the last century are the installation of pews to replace the chairs and a new, smaller font cover. The brass candelabra in the choir remain, although now converted from gas to electricity.

*Left:* Even in black and white, Conway's picture of the garden at Horsley Court is evocative, although one cannot help wishing that colour photography had been invented earlier.

*Below:* Conway's picture of the roadway and entrance to Horsley Court.

Two contrasting views of Washpool, with its stone tank for sheep dipping – the reason for the hamlet's name. The top picture, taken around 1920, looks towards Horsley Church and village, while the bottom picture, a postcard written in 1916, looks in the opposite direction up the lane towards Barton End and the Bath Road. Note the thatched cottage in the distance.

Horsley Brass Band in the 1920s. The names of the musicians are believed to be, from left to right, back row: -?-, Bert Stevens, Alf Moon, Harry Chew. Third row: -?-, George Jones, Harry Saunders, Lawrence Jones, Charlie White. Second row: Wilf Gardiner, Jack Allway, Fred Malpass, Bert Sawyer, Bert Williams. Front row: Bill White, Vince Gardiner, Walt Farmiloe, Fred Halliday junior, Fred Halliday senior, Walter Vick, Arthur Dyer.

*Opposite above and below:* A group of three superb pictures of Washpool, dating from around 1900, has recently been deposited at the Nailsworth Town Archive. Two have been chosen for inclusion in this book. The first image (*above*) is a fine study of country life. In it a workman tidies the verge at the side of the road. In the second photograph (*below*) note the pigs in the foreground.

Horsley AFC Third Division Stroud League cup winners, 1926/27. From left to right, back row:
C. Burge, A. Symons, A. Jones, A. Stevens, M. Allen, D.W.H. Skrine (president), F. Sawyer (captain),
F. Malpas, T. Kent, H. Chew, H. Tainton (trainer). Middle row: A. Walkley, N. Walkley (groundsman),
A. Harvey, W. Minett, C. Drew, F. Totterdale, E. Pride, G. Dyer, E. Wheeler. Front row: P. Harvey, F. Allway
(vice-captain), T. Harvey, R. Fletcher, H. Harvey, M. Vick, S. Hudd, (mascot).

*Opposite above:* The community of Hartley Bridge consists of a handful of houses a few hundred yards
out of Horsley village. The unidentified lady appears on several similar photographs of different locations
around Nailsworth (see page 50).

*Opposite below:* Downend is a sizeable hamlet situated up a side valley from the Nailsworth to Horsley
road. It once boasted a public house, The White Hart, kept in 1910 by S.G. Bingle.

Hartley Bridge.

Downend. Horsley. Glos.

# Other local titles published by Tempus

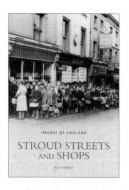

## Stroud Streets and Shops
WILF MERRETT

With over 150 photographs, postcards and advertisements, *Stroud Streets and Shops* captures the town's commercial heritage. At the beginning of the twentieth century, there were a number of shops in Stroud offering everything the casual shopper or housewife needed. The town has seen many changes since then and this book recalls Stroud in the days before the arrival of supermarkets and shopping malls.

0 7524 3307 5

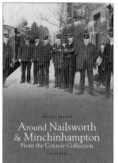

## Around Nailsworth and Minchinhampton
HOWARD BEARD

This pocket-sized selection of photographs from the collection of photographer E.P. Conway provides a social history of Nailsworth and Minchinhampton at the beginning of the twentieth century. Street scenes, carnivals, church parades, portraits and other images all offer a glimpse into the secure tranquillity of Edwardian England.

1 845 88189 3

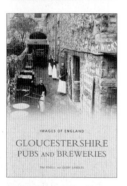

## Gloucestershire Pubs and Breweries
TIM EDGELL AND GEOFF SANDLES

Illustrated with over 200 old photographs, postcards and promotional advertisements, this absorbing collection offers the reader an insight into Gloucestershire's pubs and breweries past and present. Included are images of the Cheltenham Original Brewery, Cainscross Brewery, Nailsworth Brewery and the Stroud Brewery Company, as well as many snapshots of local pubs and landlords.

0 7524 3524 8

## Folklore of Gloucestershire
ROY PALMER

Here are recounted tales inspired by landscape, village lore, legends, superstitions, stories of devils, fairies, witches and ghosts, sports and fairs, song and dance, revels and rituals. Roy Palmer is an acknowledged authority on the subject of folklore, and his work in collecting material from within the traditional boundaries of Gloucestershire is a major contribution to the historic records of the county.

0 7524 2246 4

If you are interested in purchasing other books published by Tempus, or in case you have difficulty finding any Tempus books in your local bookshop, you can also place orders directly through our website

**www.tempus-publishing.com**